JAN '99

D0689802

DATE DUE

SEP 2 2 2003	MAY 0 7 2005	
JAN 3 2004	JUL 0 9 2005	
	DEC 1 0 2005	
MAR 3 1 2004	AUG 1 3 2008	
MAY 1 2 2004		
MAY 1 2 2004	SEP 2 3 2009	
	OCT 0 2 2010	
AUG 2 1 2004		
NOV 1 2 2004		
DEC 2 2 2004		
JAN 0 9 2005		
APR 1 0 2005		
APR 2 3 2005		
DEC 1 6 2007		
APR 0 6 2008		

Brodart Co. Cat. # 55 137 001 Printed in USA

Looking at . . . Pachycephalosaurus
A Dinosaur from the CRETACEOUS Period

THE NEW DINOSAUR COLLECTION

For a free color catalog describing Gareth Stevens' list of high-quality books,
call 1-800-542-2595 (USA) or 1-800-461-9120 (Canada).
Gareth Stevens' Fax: (414) 225-0377.

Library of Congress Cataloging-in-Publication Data

Freedman, Frances.
    Looking at—Pachycephalosaurus / written by Frances Freedman; illustrated by Tony Gibbons.
— North American ed.
        p. cm. — (The New dinosaur collection)
    Includes index.
    ISBN 0-8368-1277-8
    1. Pachycephalosaurus—Juvenile literature. [1. Pachycephalosaurus. 2. Dinosaurs.]
    I. Gibbons, Tony, ill. II. Title. III. Title: Pachycephalosaurus. IV. Series.
QE862.O65F74 1995
567.9′7—dc20   94-37773

This North American edition first published in 1995 by
Gareth Stevens Publishing
1555 North RiverCenter Drive, Suite 201
Milwaukee, Wisconsin 53212 USA

This U.S. edition © 1995 by Gareth Stevens, Inc. Created with original © 1994 by Quartz
Editorial Services, Premier House, 112 Station Road, Edgware HA8 7AQ U.K.

Consultant: Dr. David Norman, Director of the Sedgwick Museum of Geology,
University of Cambridge, England.

Additional artwork by Clare Herronneau.

All rights reserved. No part of this book may be reproduced, stored in a retrieval
system, or transmitted in any form or by any means, electronic, mechanical,
photocopying, or otherwise, without the prior written permission of the
copyright holder.

Printed in the United States of America

1 2 3 4 5 6 7 8 9 99 98 97 96 95

GLASGOW CITY · COUNTY LIBRARY

Looking at . . . Pachycephalosaurus
A Dinosaur from the CRETACEOUS Period

by Frances Freedman

Illustrated by Tony Gibbons

Gareth Stevens Publishing
MILWAUKEE

Contents

Introducing Pachycephalosaurus

Just look
at this
amazing beast!
Its head is like
a crash helmet with lots
of bumpy pieces of bone
around it, and it belongs on
the body of **Pachycephalosaurus**
(PAK-EE-SEFF-A-LOW-SAW-RUS). This
bizarre dinosaur lived about
70 million years ago, in
Cretaceous times.

First discovered in 1940 by
William Winkley in Montana,
Pachycephalosaurus
has a name meaning
"thick-headed
reptile."

Paleontologists —
scientists who study
the remains of
prehistoric life —
have discovered
some intriguing
facts about this
creature. Read on
to find out about
the strange habits of
this dinosaur.

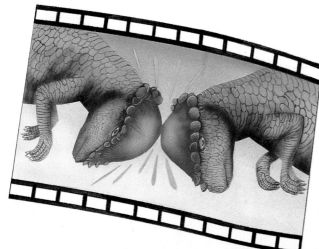

Thick-skulled dinosaur

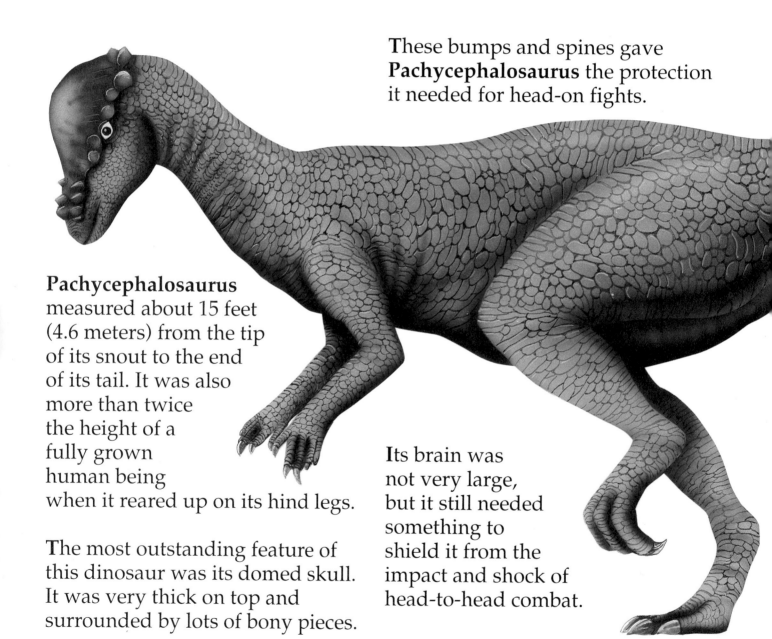

These bumps and spines gave **Pachycephalosaurus** the protection it needed for head-on fights.

Pachycephalosaurus measured about 15 feet (4.6 meters) from the tip of its snout to the end of its tail. It was also more than twice the height of a fully grown human being when it reared up on its hind legs.

The most outstanding feature of this dinosaur was its domed skull. It was very thick on top and surrounded by lots of bony pieces.

Its brain was not very large, but it still needed something to shield it from the impact and shock of head-to-head combat.

6

However, **Pachycephalosaurus** did not go out of its way to attack and kill other dinosaurs. It was a plant-eater and did not need to kill other creatures for food. Instead, the males sparred with each other over mates and territory.

It also used its skull as a battering ram if carnivorous (meat-eating) dinosaurs attacked it for a meal of raw **Pachycephalosaurus**.

Pachycephalosaurus's thick skull, therefore, had to withstand an enormous amount of bashing.

Just as it's a good idea to wear a helmet when riding a bike, so **Pachycephalosaurus** found its tough skull a very useful protection.

Some scientists also believe the males may have had more brightly colored heads than the females. This made the males very attractive to the opposite sex.

Here, then, are the points to look for if you go **Pachycephalosaurus**-spotting in a museum:
- a very thick, domed, armored skull
- shorter front limbs than hind legs
- wide hips
- a long, straight tail

Sturdy skeleton

Pachycephalosaurus, as you can see, stood on two back legs and had two short front limbs.

This meant that the force of the blows they struck could be absorbed by their thick necks, shoulders, and backbones.

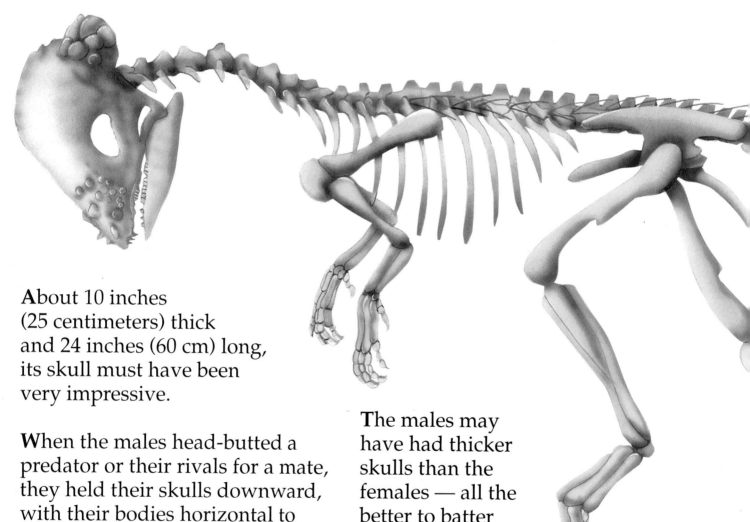

About 10 inches (25 centimeters) thick and 24 inches (60 cm) long, its skull must have been very impressive.

When the males head-butted a predator or their rivals for a mate, they held their skulls downward, with their bodies horizontal to the ground.

The males may have had thicker skulls than the females — all the better to batter each other.

They probably chased each other before fighting. The impact would have been very strong and loud as they crashed.

Pachycephalosaurus held its long, tapering tail out stiffly behind as it ran, for better balance. Its hips, meanwhile, near the top of its back legs, were quite wide and helped strengthen its backbone.

Large eye sockets give us the clue that **Pachycephalosaurus** may have had sharp eyesight, helping it spot any sign of danger.

Most whole dinosaur skulls are rare. This is because they were usually lightweight and broke easily over all the millions of years they lay buried. But whole skulls of **Pachycephalosaurus** and its relatives are fairly common because they were so thick.

Some of today's creatures that fight head-to-head (mountain sheep, for example) have special spaces in their skulls to dull the shock to the brain when they fight. **Pachycephalosaurus**, however, had no such spaces in its skull roof. Scientists think the strong backbone absorbed much of the shock of head-butting. Otherwise, constantly using its head as a battering ram would have been very painful. Ouch!

Skeletons of **Pachycephalosaurus** have been found only in North America, while those of its relatives have been dug up there and in Asia. One fragment of a relative's domed, armored skull has also recently been discovered in Madagascar, off the southeastern coast of Africa. This dinosaur was named **Majungatholus** (MA-YUNG-A-THO-LUS) after the area of its discovery. **Majungatholus** is the first relative of **Pachycephalosaurus** found in the Southern Hemisphere.

9

Amazing

Pachycephalosaurus (1) was not the only dinosaur to have an odd-looking head. Let's meet some others and discover how bizarre they were.

Triceratops (TRY-SER-A-TOPS) (2) was known for its three horns, two above the eyes and one on its nose. This 30-foot (9-m)-long herbivore had a snout shaped like a parrot's beak. This snout was used for slicing leaves and other vegetation.

2

1

Behind its two larger, upper horns, **Triceratops** also had a frill that framed its face and had a wavy edge. Its head alone was sometimes the size of a very tall man — imagine that!

heads

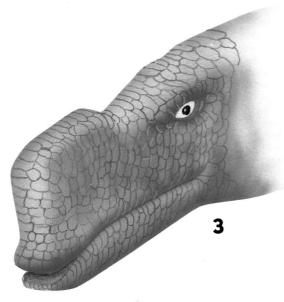

3

Fifty-foot (15-m)-long **Lambeosaurus** (<u>LAM</u>-BEE-OH-<u>SAW</u>-RUS) (**5**) had a skull with a peculiar, hatchet-shaped, hollow crest.

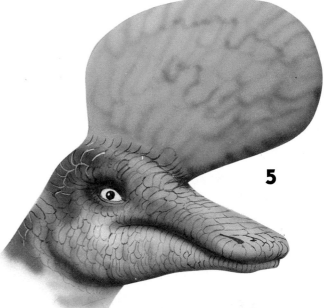

5

Now take a look at **Chirostenotes** (<u>KY</u>-ROW-<u>STEN</u>-OH-<u>TEEZ</u>) (**3**). Its head had a long, deep beak and a bulging upper jaw. What a strange creature!

Tsintaosaurus (<u>SINT</u>-OW-<u>SAW</u>-RUS) (**4**) was a large, duck-billed plant-eater with an odd, hollow horn pointing forward on its head.

4

Scientists think this crest was larger in the males than it was in the females.

If humans had been around at the time of the dinosaurs, it might have been very scary to come face-to-face with any of these creatures!

Prizefighters

It was a bright morning in Cretaceous times, and most of the creatures living in what is now known as North America were just stirring. All was peaceful apart from the occasional rustle caused by a dinosaur as it prepared itself for the day ahead.

Thwack! Thwack! Again and again, the terrible sound echoed all around. They were fighting over the females browsing lower down the slopes, almost unaware of what was going on.

Suddenly, a deafening noise came from the slopes of a mountain. Two male **Pachycephalosaurus** were having a head-banging match.

The force with which the two **Pachycephalosaurus** hit each other was tremendous. The match continued for a full five minutes. Elsewhere on the mountain slopes, other males were having similar competitions.

All of them were **Pachycephalosaurus**. No other dinosaurs in the area had bony skulls suitable for fighting with their heads in this way over mates. Male **Triceratops**, however, used their horns in

Both **Pachycephalosaurus** were of similar size and strength. Which would be the victor?

Eventually, exhausted, one of the dinosaurs decided it would give in. It had had enough.

It turned away and lumbered off, somewhat dazed. The other male had won the day.

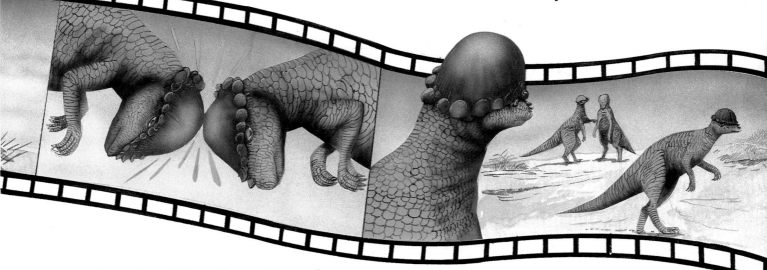

head-to-head battles when they fought over females.

It seemed the fight between the tough, angry boneheads would never end.

This would now be *his* territory, and *he* would mate with the nearby females.

Mountain

Scientists believe
Pachycephalosaurus probably
lived in mountain areas in
groups, out of the reach of giant
Cretaceous predators such
as **Tyrannosaurus rex**
(TIE-<u>RAN</u>-OH-<u>SAW</u>-RUS <u>RECKS</u>).

14

plant-eaters

Most of the skulls of **Pachycephalosaurus** have been found in valleys, however. Experts think they did not live there but that the skulls had probably been washed downstream to these lowlands.

Pachycephalosaurus had small teeth that were rough-edged, like a steak knife. These were well-suited to cutting through tough vegetation.

Pachycephalosaurus probably ate several times a day, enjoying seeds, leaves, and twigs. All those head-banging matches required a lot of energy, so large meals were very important.

15

Did you know . . . ?

Dinosaurs are certainly fascinating creatures, and we all have lots of questions to ask about them. Here are the experts' answers to some of the most common questions.

How long did dinosaurs rule the world?

Around 65 million years ago, dinosaurs suddenly became extinct. Most scientists agree that a giant meteorite hit Earth, blotting out the sun for a long while and probably causing dinosaurs to starve to death. The mighty dinosaurs existed on our planet for some 160 million years in all — that's much longer than humans have existed.

What are coprolites?

Coprolites are fossilized dung or droppings. Scientists can tell from them the sort of diet a particular dinosaur had. Did it eat only plants, for instance, or are there traces of broken bones or teeth in the coprolites that show it was a carnivore?

Could one type of dinosaur breed with another kind?

Scientists think this is very unlikely. After all, only a few creatures ever interbreed.

So one **Pachycephalosaurus** probably only mated with another **Pachycephalosaurus**, and not with an **Anatotitan** (AN-AT-OH-TIE-TAN), for instance.

How many kinds of dinosaurs were there?

So far, paleontologists have found about one thousand different types of dinosaurs. The remains have been discovered all over the world, and there may have been more.

Some dinosaurs haven't even been found yet, while the remains of others may never be found.

What was a dinosaur's life span?

No one is sure how long dinosaurs lived, but scientists are trying to find out by studying the growth rate of the dinosaur bones.

It is difficult for experts to determine age because so many dinosaurs did not live a full life span, having been attacked by others for food.

But it seems that a dinosaur like **Massospondylus** (MASS-OH-SPOND-EE-LUS), *below*, which lived about 220 million years ago, had a life span of up to 70 years — much like humans today.

17

A puzzle still to be solved

All mammals are warm-blooded, and that includes *you*. Reptiles, however, are cold-blooded. So what about dinosaurs? Some scientists think dinosaurs must have been cold-blooded, like today's reptiles.

If they were cold-blooded, dinosaurs had to actively participate in raising or lowering their body temperature. They may have done this by moving in and out of the sun, just as today's cold-blooded reptiles do. Some dinosaurs such as **Stegosaurus** (STEG-OH-SAW-RUS) (**1**) may have used the plates on their backs to help them warm up or cool down. They may even have been able to move these plates up and down to help with this.

Scientists even think the plates were used like solar panels to absorb heat from the sun.

1

The sail on **Ouranosaurus**'s (OO-RAN-OH-SAW-RUS) (**2**) back may also have been used for the same purpose. If it was too hot, **Ouranosaurus** could lose heat through its sail. And if it got cold, it could absorb the sun's heat this way.

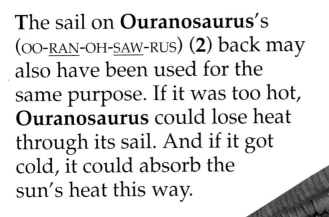

However, we know that many dinosaurs could run for great distances and at a high speed — **Gallimimus** (GAL-EE-MIME-US) (**3**), for instance. Today's reptiles, however, can only move in shorter bursts because they are cold-blooded and do not have enough energy.

So were dinosaurs warm-blooded, after all? If they were warm-blooded, their body temperature would be maintained automatically, just like today's birds and mammals.

No one knows for sure yet. Perhaps some dinosaurs were cold-blooded and others warm-blooded. This puzzle is even more complex because of all the different types of dinosaurs that once existed.

Pachycephalosaurus

Several obvious physical features would have helped you spot a **Pachycephalosaurus** if you had lived in Cretaceous times.

Crash-helmet skull

As you know, it's a sensible idea to wear a crash helmet when riding a bicycle or when horseback riding, in case of an accident. **Pachycephalosaurus** had a built-in protection in its thick, dome-shaped, and knobby head. You can see its skull below.

Bright coloring

Scientists think the male **Pachycephalosaurus** may have had a brightly colored head. This would have attracted the less colorful females.

Such color differences exist in many animals today. The peacock, for example, has much more colorful feathers than its mate, the peahen.

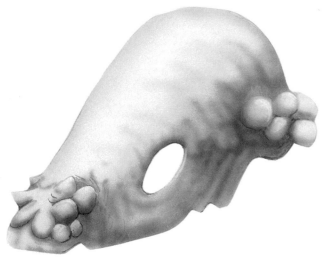

data

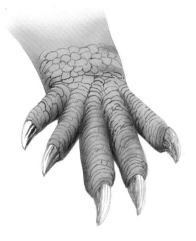

Five-fingered hands

Pachycephalosaurus had five-fingered hands with claws that helped it grasp and break off plants to eat.

Tapering tail

Pachycephalosaurus probably walked with its tail, which was stiff and thin toward the tip, held out straight behind it.

Wide hips

Some dinosaurs had such wide hips that a few scientists have wondered whether they may have given birth to live young, like mammals do, rather than laying eggs. However, it is most likely that all dinosaurs laid eggs, although we have yet to find any laid by **Pachycephalosaurus**.

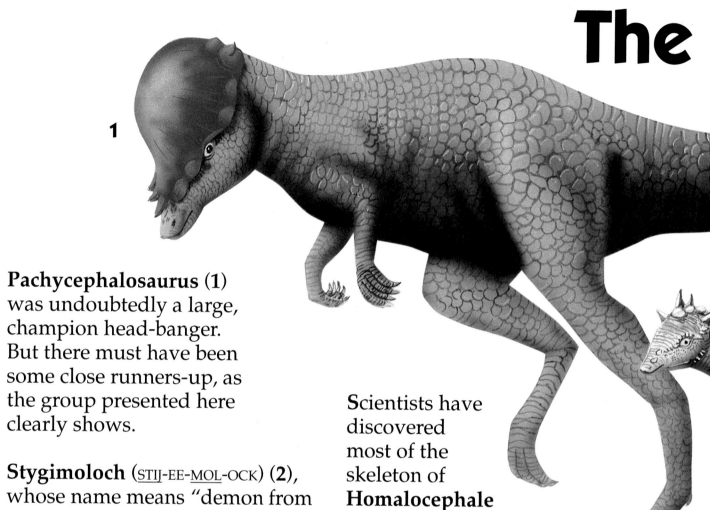

Pachycephalosaurus (1) was undoubtedly a large, champion head-banger. But there must have been some close runners-up, as the group presented here clearly shows.

Stygimoloch (S̲T̲I̲J̲-EE-M̲O̲L̲-OCK) **(2)**, whose name means "demon from the River Styx," is a recent find. It was about 10 feet (3 m) long and lived in North America in Late Cretaceous times. Its domed skull had decorative bony horns and spikes that also protected its brain.

Homalocephale (HOM-A̲L̲-OH-K̲E̲F̲-A̲L̲-EE) **(3)** was another Late Cretaceous dinosaur, this time from Mongolia.

Scientists have discovered most of the skeleton of **Homalocephale** and know it was about 10 feet (3 m) long. Also a plant-eater, **Homalocephale** had a flatter head than the rest of the thick-skulled gang. Its head was also covered in bony knobs along the back, but the roof of its skull was fairly smooth.

bonehead gang

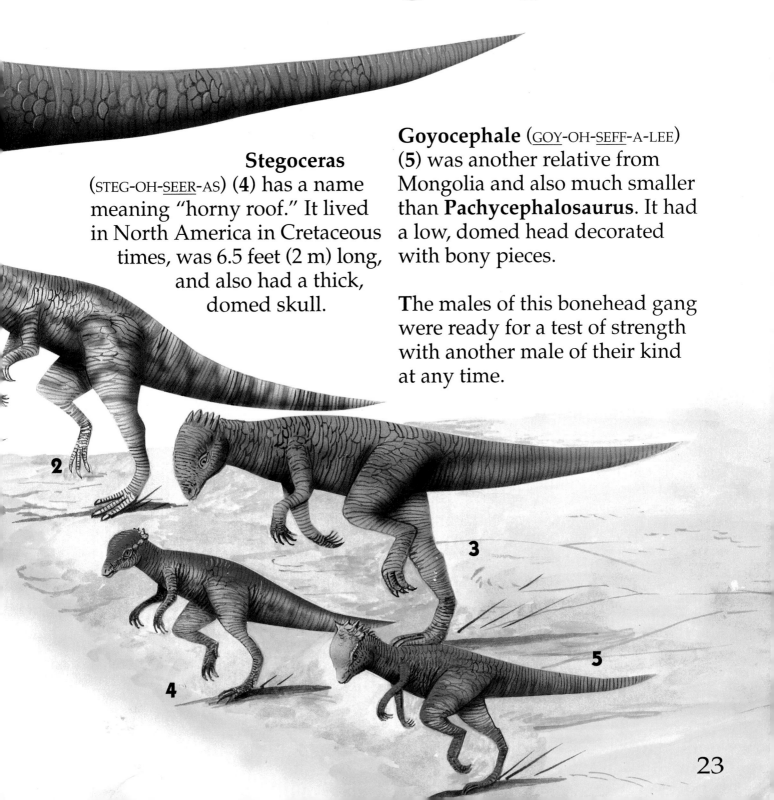

Stegoceras (STEG-OH-SEER-AS) **(4)** has a name meaning "horny roof." It lived in North America in Cretaceous times, was 6.5 feet (2 m) long, and also had a thick, domed skull.

Goyocephale (GOY-OH-SEFF-A-LEE) **(5)** was another relative from Mongolia and also much smaller than **Pachycephalosaurus**. It had a low, domed head decorated with bony pieces.

The males of this bonehead gang were ready for a test of strength with another male of their kind at any time.

GLOSSARY

carnivores — meat-eating animals.

extinction — the dying out of all members of a plant or animal species.

herbivores — plant-eating animals.

mate — (n) a partner or one member of a pair; (v) to join (animals) together to produce young.

meteorites — chunks of rock from space that reach Earth before burning up completely.

paleontologists — scientists who study the remains of plants and animals that lived millions of years ago.

predators — animals that capture and kill other animals for food.

remains — a skeleton, bones, or a dead body.

reptiles — cold-blooded animals that have hornlike or scale-covered skin.

snout — protruding nose and jaws of an animal.

INDEX